BUSH
SIXTEEN STONE TOUR

All photographs by Peter Black

Written by Peter Martin

Dedication

To my father, Noel Black

Lyrics reproduced by kind permission of
Gavin Rossdale/Mad Dog Winston Music Ltd.

Thanks...Lisa, Gavin, Nigel, Dave, Robin, Dave Dorrell Management (David, Claudia, Sam), Trauma, Giant, Interscope, MCA, Rob Kahane, Paul Palmer, Ross, Clint, Dale, Raz, Bone, Bill, Cristal, Alex Room Service Tate, Sarah, Belinda, Tom, Sue, Renshaw, Little Linus, John and Kathy, Little Charlie, David & Margot, Kane & Bruce, Jemima, Lily, Dewi & Eden, Max, Ella &, last but not least, Winston.

Order No. OP 47889
US International Standard Book Number: 0.8256.1601.8
UK International Standard Book Number: 0.7119.6341.X

Exclusive Distributors:
Music Sales Corporation
257 Park Avenue South, New York, NY 10010 USA
Music Sales Limited
8/9 Frith Street, London W1V 5TZ England
Music Sales Pty. Limited
120 Rothschild Street, Rosebery, Sydney, NSW 2018, Australia

Printed in the United States of America by
Vicks Lithograph and Printing Corporation

OMNIBUS PRESS
LONDON · NEW YORK · SYDNEY

SEX (*see common vernacular for female pubic hair*)
DRUGS (*see common vernacular for marijuana*)
ROCK'N'ROLL (*see multi-million selling English band*)
POLITICS (*see George*)...

Whatever the connotation BUSH has indelibly stained itself on the modern collective American consciousness.

Meanwhile, at the beginning of 1995, the 4 members of Bush - Robin Goodridge (drums), Dave Parsons (bass), Nigel Pulsford (guitar), Gavin Rossdale (guitar/vocals) - had not sold a solitary record and anxiously rehearsed for The Sixteen Stone Tour in a dark, dank, Dickensian basement in freezing, monochromatic London.

From those tentative rehearsals on the eve of their first US tour to the virtual anonymity of their early club dates back in January '95, it didn't take long for The Sixteen Stone Tour to create Bush fever.

By June 14 of that year "Sixteen Stone" had sold one million copies as the tour escalated from intimate club venues to small arenas.

By the end of 1995 Bush had sold a phenomenal 3 million copies of "Sixteen Stone" and clocked top 10 hits in the US Billboard singles chart, courtesy of saturation play on alternative rock radio and MTV.

INTRODUCTION

Bush experienced media overload in 1996 with Gavin posing partially naked on the cover of Rolling Stone's fastest selling issue of the year. Appearances on the Christmas radio concerts for KROQ in Los Angeles and Z100 in New York were followed by prestigious slots on Howard Stern, David Letterman, The Tonight Show and Saturday Night Live.

Bush capped off their gruelling 230 date US tour with sell out summer dates at the legendary Red Rocks Stadium in Denver, Colorado, pushing "Sixteen Stone" forward a massive 5 million sales.

Since the completion of The Sixteen Stone Tour the band were awarded the ultimate industry accolade, The 1996 MTV Viewers Choice Award for Best Video for "Glycerine".

"Sixteen Stone" has since sold over 7 million copies in the States generating five consecutive top ten Billboard hit singles ("Everything Zen", "Little Things", "Comedown", "Glycerine" and "Machinehead").

Sixteen Stone Tour Book is a document of Bush's record-breaking 1995/96 tour, comprising black & white photographs taken by London-based photographer Peter Black and irreverent text from writer Peter Martin. The book tracks Bush from those early rehearsals in London to Red Rocks in the summer of '96.

*Stop Press...As this book goes to bed the second Bush album "Razorblade Suitcase" enters the Billboard charts at No.1 with a bullet, knocking Interscope labelmate Snoop Doggy Dogg off the top spot with a staggering 293,586 sales in its first week of release. The story continues...

Deep in the heart of Dickensian London, a fresh faced Bush rehearse for the first Sixteen Stone tour of the States.

TERMINAL STUDIOS, BLACKFRIARS BRIDGE, LONDON. JAN.1.95.

Although LA radio station K-ROQ were heavily plugging the record, at this point its sales were less than zero.

Nigel angelically rehearses for the first US Bush tour,

innocent of the satanic rock 'n' roll excess that awaits him.

TERMINAL STUDIOS, BLACKFRIARS BRIDGE, LONDON. JAN.2.95.

An exile on main street.

NEW ORLEANS, LA. MAR.14.95.

Come all ye stage divers

RANDONN INN, NEW ORLEANS, LA. MAR.14.95.

AMERICA'S MOST WANTED.

A strange man wearing a black woollen hat and dark glasses was seen casing the Wells Fargo Bank last Wednesday at around 3.00. If you have seen this man please contact your local police force. Although not armed he is scary.

DOWNTOWN HOUSTON, TX. MAR.15.95.

7:30 in the am
Robin and Dave wonder if. . .

the truth is out there

TRUCK STOP, MILWAUKEE, WI. MAY.29.95.

The day Sixteen Stone passed 500,000 sales Gavin signs on the dotted line as the tour bus offloads the contents of its chemical toilet onto the forecourt

COMFORT INN, AUSTIN, TX. MAR.16.95.

Robin freezes his bollocks off outside the local replica ancient Roman village

THE RAVE, MILWAUKEE, WI. MAR.19.95.

"I don't believe that Elvis is dead."

Leaving Graceland,
Nigel contemplates the true fate of The King.

"you wanna see my peccadillos, hot dog 7.30 in the morning and I'm big into war"

2 minutes into "Machinehead" power out at the 25,000 capacity Livestock 5. Bush repair backstage to make inevitable Spinal Tap dead drummer joke.

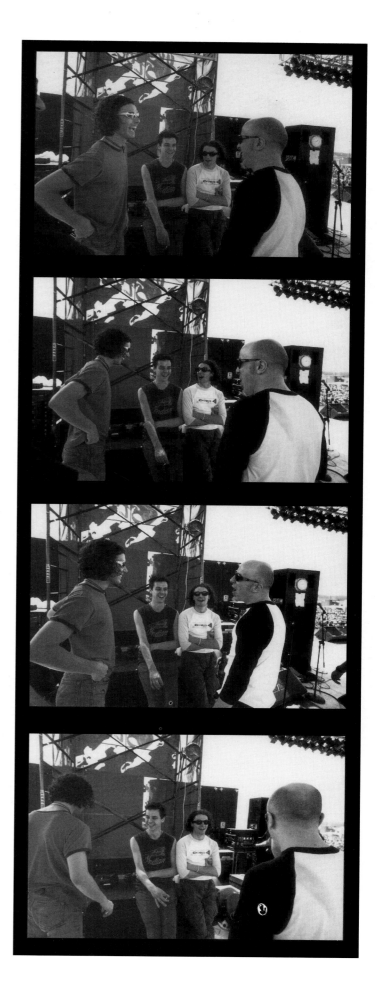

"I don't want this, remember that"

BUFFALO ARMORY, BUFFALO, NY. JUN.1.95.

DARK STAR

WETLANDS, NEW YORK CITY, NY. MAR.6.95.

"I'm never alone, I'm alone all the time"

NEW ROCK FEST, MARCUS AMPHITHEATRE, MILWAUKEE, WI. MAY.29.95.

violencesex

"there's no sex in your violence"

sex
violence
sex
violence
violence

Gavin protects his modesty in the underground armoury.

BUFFALO US ARMORY, BUFFALO, NY. JUN.1.95.

Dave learns another chord (that makes 4 kids, count 'em!)

CAPRI MUSIC HALL, CHARLOTTE, N.C. MAY.14.95.

strangely resonant of a popular rock film parody,
Bush continue their search for the stage in this US military complex

BUFFALO ARMORY, BUFFALO, NY. JUN.1.95.

The Father,

The Son,

and The Holy Ghost

NEW ROCK FEST, MARCUS AMPHITHEATRE, MILWAUKEE, WI. MAY.29.95.

On the way back to their apartment, the 1853 gothic railway conversion atop
the local shopping mall, our photographer Mr. Pete Black, accompanied by 50%
of Bush, was stalked by a crazed, albeit, confused fan.

                              THE FAN
               I saw you on-stage. You're the photographer.

                          THE PHOTOGRAPHER
                                Yes.

                              THE FAN
                  Can I come back and meet the band?

                          THE PHOTOGRAPHER
              Sure you can. Which one of them do you want to meet?

                              THE FAN
                             All of them!

                          THE PHOTOGRAPHER
                       Would Dave and Nigel do?

                              THE FAN
                               Yeah!

At which point 50% of BUSH turn around and make themselves known to THE
   FAN. THE FAN doesn't believe they are who they say they are. DAVE,
      incredulously, is forced to show THE FAN his credentials.

                              THE FAN
                            Oh my word!

UNION STATION, INDIANAPOLIS, IN. MAR.17.95.

"*Lazy day on a darker breed.*"

BUFFALO U.S. ARMOURY. BUFFALO, NY. JUN.1.95.

"*leaning on my conscience Wall, blood is like Wine, unconscious all the time*"

THE GARAGE, HIGHBURY, LONDON. JUN.26.95.

by the light of the stereo waltz"

"in silence we still talk,

SAVAGE HALL, UNIVERSITY OF TOLEDO, TOLEDO, OH. MAR.1.96.

"thick skinned - cities you drive me through"

320 PERFORMANCE, NASHVILLE, TN. MAR.22.95.

Waiting for the Man

Gavin on the set of the "Machinehead" video.

WEDGEWOOD ROOMS, PORTSMOUTH. NOV.21.95.

Whatever

RFK STADIUM, WASHINGTON DC. JUN.3.95.

"*flicker on a tv screen*

everything's more than it seems".

Nigel imagines the horrific court case in store for our photographer in the eventuality of this photograph being used in a forthcoming book.

UNION STATION, INDIANAPOLIS, IN. MAR.17.95.

Dave considers the inherent dangers of getting off the bus.

LEE'S PALACE, TORONTO, CANADA. FEB.25.95.

TESTOSTERONE

THE STING, NEW BRITAIN, CT. JUN.2.95.

Nigel is wearing sunglasses by Local Truck Stop (Model's own)
Gavin is wearing a casual top by Fred Perry and jeans by Brutus (model's own)
Available at all good fashion boutiques

HARTFORD, CT. JUN.2.95.

Dale (guitar tech) and Clint (production manager)

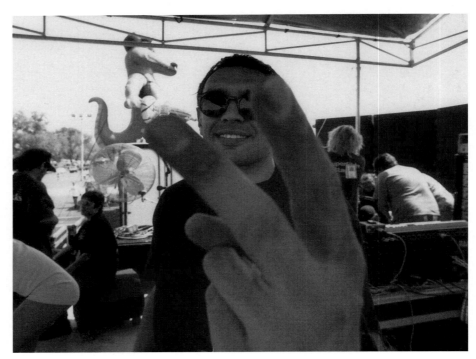

Raz (monitor engineer)

MEMORIAL AUDITORIUM, GREENVILLE, S.C. FEB.18.96.

Let's hear it for the official Sixteen Stone tour crew photo! (L-R)
Back Row: Dave (bass/irony & good humour), Clint (production manager),
Bone (driver/bodyguard), Dave L (sound engineer).
Middle: Robin (drums/sarcasm & slapstick humour), Bobby (guitar tech),
Nigel (guitar/cynicism & general raconteur), Raz (monitor engineer).
Front: Gary (tour manager) Gavin (vocals/guitar & no apparent sense of humour)

"I'M AN ALIEN

YOU'RE AN ALIEN."

SOUTH BEACH. MIAMI, FL. MAR.27.95

This ain't no Disco

CAMEO THEATER, MIAMI, FL. MAR.27.95.

SLEEP BUSH, THINK BUSH,

DRINK BUSH, EAT BUSH.

URBAN ART BAR, HOUSTON, TX. MAR.15.95.

Bush celebrate their Independence.

Dead Ringers

LIVESTOCK 5, TAMPA, FL. MAR.26.95.

Pre-Pukkelpop Dave takes a slide down the Darwinian chain of evolution.

HOTEL, OUTSIDE BRUSSELS, BELGIUM. AUG.24.96.

Nigel, fresh from slicing a finger open, drinks a cold one to kill the pain.
Robin looks duly concerned.

Gavin signs his life away.

.IVESTOCK 5, TAMPA, FL. MAR.26.95.

Below: tour manager Gary Basili (left) and Gavin.

Robin, bodyguard Bone (centre) and Nigel.

APOCALYPSE NOW

The band played Wagner's "Ride of the Valkyries" over
their external tannoy system to announce their arrival.

Nigel pulls a stocking over his head on the Bush Access All Areas laminate
in a cunning attempt to foil the stringent new security measures.

for hands that do dishes

WINSTON, SALEM, N.C. FEB.23.96.

Imagine the sound of a guitar solo over a wall of amplification

FLOAT RIGHT PARK, SOMERSET, WI. MAY.28.95.

Nigel attempts his legendary out-of-focus mime routine.
Gavin, somewhat overdressed, does his best to ignore him.

"the mighty backward fall,
stare at the lights on the wall"

BUZZARD PALOOZA, CUYAHOGA FALLS, OH. MAY.21.95.

DAZED & CONFUSED

DAZED

CONFUSED

CONFUSED

CONFUSED

DAZED

ASTORIA 2, LONDON. DEC.1.95.

"We rise - lose it on oblivion"

320 PERFORMANCE, NASHVILLE, TN. MAR.22.95.

YOKELMANIA

FLEECE AND FIRKIN, BRISTOL. NOV.29.95.

YOU LOOKIN' AT ME?

YOU LOOKIN' AT ME?   YOU LOOKIN' AT ME?

YOU LOOKIN' AT ME?

YOU LOOKIN' AT ME?

YOU LOOKIN' AT ME?

OOKIN' AT

LIVESTOCK 5 FESTIVAL, TAMPA, FL. MAR.26.95.

A rare shot of Robin losing his rug

THE PALACE, DETROIT, MI. FEB.28.96.

Yogurt, Towel, Chair, Set List, Drum Stick, Lighter, Beer on Formica

"you come alone on a mass attack"

POINTFEST, RIVERPORT AMPHITHEATRE, ST. LOUIS, MO. MAY.26.95.

ANIMAL

HORNET'S TRAINING CENTER, CHARLOTTE, N.C. FEB.24.96.

PRETTY VACANT

OUTSIDE THE REGENCY, SPRINGFIELD, MO. MAR.22.95.

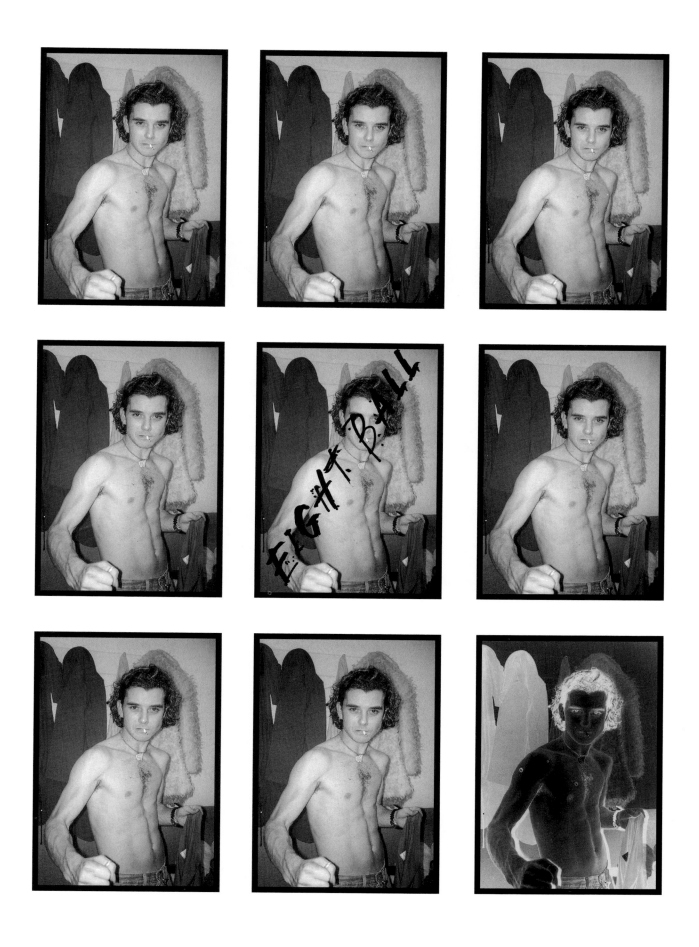

EIGHT BALL

Hand, Knee, Paper, Pen.

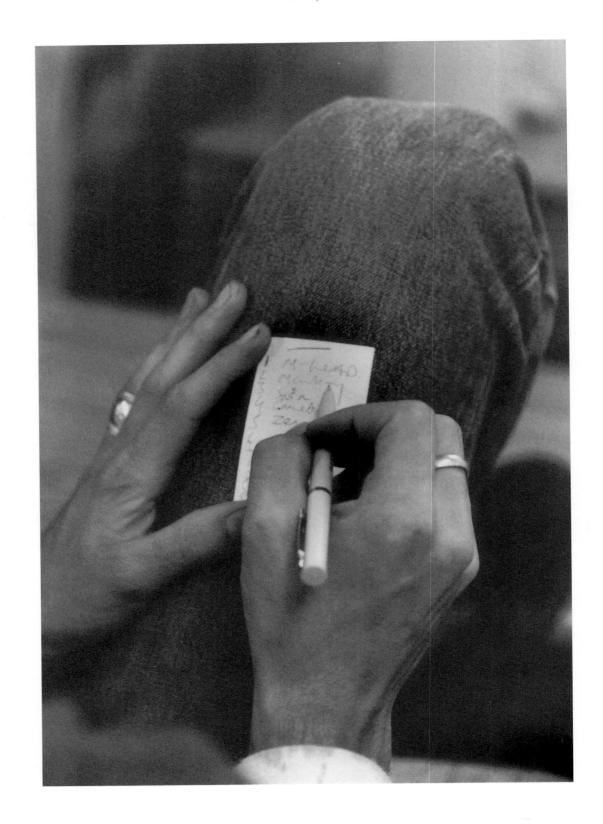

ASTORIA THEATRE, LONDON. DEC.1.95.

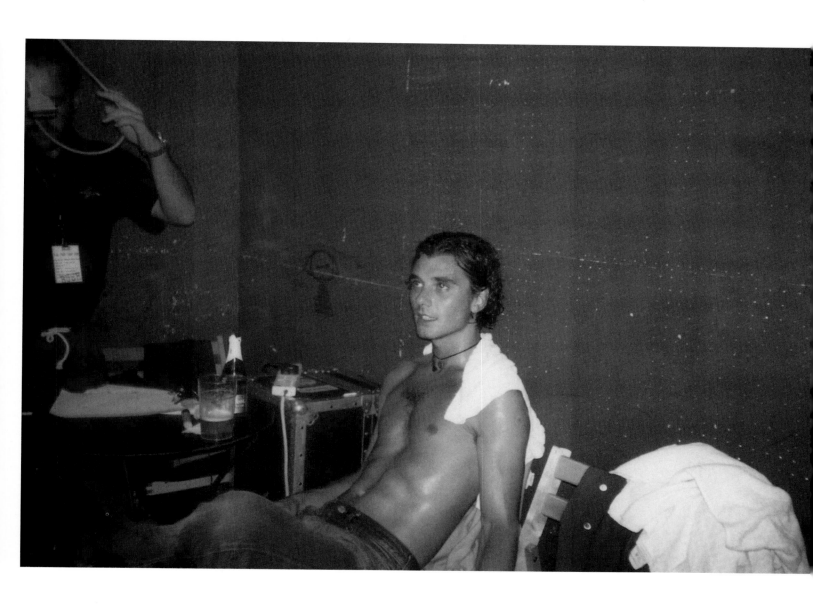

Ross (new tour manager) and Gavin take a sauna

ANARCHY IN THE UK

Bush pit mania hits mainland England

ASTORIA 2, LONDON. DEC.1.95.

Robin and Dave join Ross, now doubled up with heat exhaustion, in the sauna

KING TUTS, GLASGOW, SCOTLAND. JUN.21.95.

EVERYTH

FLOAT RIGHT PARK, SOMERSET, WI. MAY.28.95.

Crisis?

What crisis?

"deaf, dumb and thirty,

starting to deserve this"

"I am lionface, no sancho panza"

NEW ROCK FES, MARCUS AMPHITHEATRE, MILWAUKEE, WI. MAY.29.95.

Nigel gets in some early training for the Olympics

RIVAT

ATLANTA. MAY.12.95.

About to be executed for acts of treason,

our prisoner considers one last request...

OUTSIDE BUFFALO ARMORY, BUFFALO, NY. JUN.1.95.

Headless bodyguard (left) Gavin and Jasmine (right) attempt to relive their youth by sneaking into the crowd to see Duran Duran. Unfortunately a fellow Durannie spots Gavin and the 20,000 crowd descend on the pair, much to Jasmine's horror.

NEW ROCK FEST, MARCUS AMPHITHEATRE, MILWAUKEE, WI. MAY.29.95.

"Dave's on sale again"

Bush loved up on the bus with manager David Dorrell (eyes wide shut)

"We're naked again, maybe all we need is water and friends"

Sub-zero chillout in beer city

MEMORIAL AUDITORIUM, GREENVILLE, S.C. FEB.18.96.

Welcome to the Terrordome

Gavin gene-spliced with Winston in freak photo recreation of Sixteen Stone CD image.

PUKKELPOP FESTIVAL, OUTSIDE BRUSSELS, BELGIUM. AUG.24.96.

Gavin's got a great big guitar.
So, allegedly, has Nigel.

THE PALACE, DETROIT, MI. 28.2.96.

"I have no defense. I'm all that you see."

Fig's American colonial whitehouse post-skunk roadkill experience. R&R in the DMZ.

FIG'S HOUSE. RICHMOND, VA. FEB.19.96.

"I don't want to come back down from this cloud."

ASTORIA THEATRE. LONDON. DEC.1.95

"as you search for your demi-god"

LAWRENCE JOEL VETS COLISEUM, WINSTON, SALEM, N.C. FEB.23.96.

"raindogs howl for the century"

K STADIUM, WASHINGTON DC. JUN.3.95.

"I felt you like electric light"

RED ROCKS AMPHITHEATRE, DENVER, CO. MAY.4.96.

Bush salute the Red Rocks car park in a rare photo opportunity.

Another early morning Dave shot
(actually it is 2.30 in the afternoon).

CHARLOTTE, N.C. MAY.14.95.

COMEDOWN

MEMORIAL AUDITORIUM, GREENVILLE, S.C. FEB.18.96.

BOMB

BOMB BOMB BOMB

BOMB BOMB
BOMB

FLOAT RIGHT PARK, SOMERSET, WI. MAY.28.95.

"jekyll in you, brings out the wired in me"

Gavin reveals his second favourite organ

EDGE OF TOWN, BUFFALO, NY. JUN.1.95.